UPLAND PASSAGE

UPLAND PASSAGE

A Field Dog's Education

Robert F. Jones

Photographs by Bill Eppridge

FARRAR, STRAUS AND GIROUX

NEW YORK

Acknowledgments

We would like to thank the following persons for their skills, help, hospitality, and consideration in the course of bringing this book to print: Adrienne Aurichio, Bob Brown of *Sports Illustrated*, Bob Buckley and Gary Crumlish of Buckley Photo Lab, Jean Ceglowski (DVM), Louise Jones, Joe Judge and Donna Davenport of Twin Ponds Duck Club, Patricia McWilliams, Grace and Myron Morris, Bill Pekala and Sam Garcia of Nikon Professional Services, Paul Howard (DVM), Sean and Richard Donovan, Virginia Gerber, and our superb editor, Margaret Ferguson.

Excerpts of this story appeared in a slightly different form in *Sports Illustrated*.

Published simultaneously in Canada by HarperCollins*CanadaLtd*
Color separations by Imago Sales Ltd.
Printed and bound in the United States of America
by Worzalla Publishing Co.
Designed by Martha Rago
First edition, 1992

Library of Congress Cataloging-in-Publication Data
Jones, Robert F.
Upland passage: a field dog's education / Robert F. Jones ;
photographs by Bill Eppridge.   p.   cm.
1. Labrador retriever—United States—Biography.   2. Bird dogs—
United States—Biography.   3. Labrador retriever—Training.
4. Bird dogs—Training.   5. Fowling—United States.   6. Jones,
Robert R.   I. Title.
SF429.L3J63   1992   799.2′42—dc20   92-5110   CIP

These words are for Dan Gerber,
These pictures for Therese and Ep

.

It is well known that dogs are capable of smiling, and even of smiling very charmingly.
—Ivan Turgenev, *A Sportsman's Sketches*

UPLAND PASSAGE

Excerpt from a gunning diary

Date: 31 Oct. 1989, Tuesday, 12:30–2:00 p.m., 17th day afield.

Area: Shatterack Mountain, from Danny's apples to Ray's red pines.

Dogs: Luke, 11-year-old black Lab; Jake, 11-week-old yellow Lab puppy.

Weather: High 60s, rain in a.m., overcast, light SW breeze, occ. showers.

Gun: 20-gauge Winchester Model 23 double, low-base #9 shot.

Flushes: 2 grouse, 1 woodcock.

Shots: 1 at 1 woodcock; bagged.

Season total: 63 flushes in 26 hours afield (33 grouse, 30 woodcock); 22 shots fired at 18 birds, 11 bagged (3 grouse, 8 woodcock). Batting .500!

Remarks: Luke pushed a grouse uphill through the pine-and-birch thicket across from Canary Brook and flushed it at the edge of the clearing at top. Bird went out too low for a shot. We followed across through thin woods toward Danny's old apple orchard, where the grouse seemed to have pitched in. Luke ranged ahead, looking for a reflush. Jake stayed with me, about five yards ahead, his fat puppy belly plastered with mud (some of which scraped off when he dragged it over fallen tree trunks), his outsized paws scrabbling energetically in the muck for traction. About halfway to the apples, a woodcock went off under Jake's nose, twittering like a windup toy, angling L to R almost straightway. I popped it about 20 yds. out. Jake saw it fall—heard it thump down—then instinctively raced for it, his ears flapping like limp yellow wings. Luke, too, had heard the shot and seen the bird fall, and saw Jake run for the retrieve. Luke beat Jake to the woodcock—outraged at the puppy's act of lèse majesté—and picked it up in the nick of time. Luke looked straight at me, as if to say, How *could* you?—and then deliberately *crunched* the bird! Sibling rivalry? You bet. But it was Jake's first bird . . .

If life were fair, hunters and their gundogs would have identical life-spans—learning, peaking, and declining together, step for step, one man, one dog hunting along on a trail toward that Great Grouse Covert in the Sky. But it doesn't work that way. Few hardworking hunting dogs last more than a dozen seasons. Then time catches up with them, rewarding their diligence with arthritis, cataracts, cysts, tumors, and just plain old age.

But the good ones never lose their passion for the field. Nothing is sadder for the hunter than seeing his old dog, lame and white-muzzled but with his tail still going like a runaway metronome, as the man takes down his gun for an outing he knows the dog cannot endure. The dog stares up with clouded eyes, pleading.

"No, boy," the man says. "Not anymore. You stay home and rest."

It is possible to hunt successfully without a dog, just as it is possible to eat cold oatmeal. But it is also about as palatable.

Over the course of a career spanning eleven bird seasons, my grizzled black Labrador, Luke, had just gotten better and better. In Vermont, where I live, those seasons run roughly ninety days long, from the last Saturday in September through the end of the year, and they had been the high points of our lives. Luke lived for the fall, and I for the joy it gave him.

Seeing a dog learn and refine his skills as a hunter is more rewarding to me than killing a limit of upland birds—four grouse and three woodcock—every day of the season. Once Luke had learned all I could teach him about flushing and retrieving game birds, he began teaching me. I learned to trust his infallible nose, which could find birds where I wouldn't have believed they could

For eleven years, Luke had been my best and only hunting partner. Now he was suddenly old, and it was time to train another Labrador.

be. I learned to follow him, on faith alone, into the really hard country—steep, overgrown hillsides bristling with thorns; muck-bottomed marshes that can suck your boots off; blizzard-whipped apple orchards where naked branches poke at your eyes and grouse get up with a roar of wings as loud as the storm but disappear, usually, before you can raise the gun. From Luke I learned persistence, endurance, stoicism, loyalty, and not a little bit about love.

By our fifth season together—if he had been human, he would have been thirty-five years old and in his prime—I began to notice that he was flushing more birds than ever directly back to me. At first I thought it was coincidence, but I began to make note of the flush-backs in my gunning diary. Over the next six seasons, Luke flushed a total of 1,078 birds (567 woodcock, 511 ruffed grouse); 63 percent of them flew toward or past my gun.

I had always been able to tell when Luke was getting "birdy": his strong otterine tail would come up and start flailing faster; he would glance over at me, wherever I was moving through the cover, to make sure I had my eye on him; his thick coat, shiny already, seemed to light up from within and throw blue-black glints as his guard hairs rose. Starting with his fifth season, however, he added a new tactic to his repertoire. Now I noticed him purposely circling out beyond where he'd located the bird, then pussyfooting in on it, his nostrils flared as he inhaled its rich scent, to end with a pouncing rush that made the bird fly. More often than not, it flew my way.

I'd like to say my marksmanship is as good as Luke's flush-back rate, but it's not. Over the years, I've rarely hit more than 40 percent of the game birds I've shot at. When I missed, Luke would look back at me with disappointed eyes. All that work for nothing.

"Gone away, boy," I might say rather lamely.

He would merely shrug and forge on . . .

When I connected, though, he was in his element—retrieving. Sharp-eyed as always, he marked where the bird had fallen and leaped after it: into muddy swamp edges, barbed thickets of multiflora rose, dense brakes of doghair aspen or maple whips, through ice-fringed rushing brooks, even a few times in the late season into snowdrifts as deep as his shoulders. Luke always got his bird. If it was down, it was ours. There was always pride in his bearing when he brought back a bird I'd shot, and gentleness in the jaws that held it.

Once we were working through a patch of old apple trees for grouse. At the far end, Luke got birdy in some whippy brush and pushed out a woodcock. I fired just as the bird turned a corner around a big maple tree that was still in full leaf. It seemed to me that I had missed. The afternoon was hot. Luke and I were both breathing hard, so I told him, "Let's take a break." He seemed reluctant, but he sat, edgy, muttering, eager. Ten minutes later, we pushed on, around the maple tree where I'd fired at the woodcock. Luke stopped about five yards behind me, peered at the ground, then looked up at me doubtfully. "Come on," I said, a bit sharply. "Hunt 'em up, hunt 'em up!" Again he seemed to shake his head, again looked at the ground before him. I went back to where he stood. There lay the woodcock I had shot at ten minutes earlier. "Okay," I said, embarrassed. "Fetch." He fetched and gave, the ritual complete. I never loved him more. We hunted on . . .

But time—"that old bald cheater," as Ben Jonson called it— deals down and dirty with all of us. By the summer of 1989, I realized that Luke would have to hang up his bell collar pretty soon. His left shoulder was arthritic, the bounce was fading from his rear suspension, and his eyes were growing hazy blue with incipient cataracts. After all, he was eleven years old—seventy-seven in human terms. I could handle the arthritis by feeding him an aspirin wrapped in raw hamburger before we went out each day; the spring would return to his stride as the season wore on and he put more up-and-down miles behind him; his nose would make up in keenness for what his eyes had lost. More disconcerting was a new problem: over the winter and spring, he had developed a hacking, half-strangulated cough that wouldn't go away. His bark sounded broken, like a teenage boy's voice when it's changing; his breath came raspy at the best of times. Jean Ceglowski, our sure-handed local vet, X-rayed Luke's chest and throat.

"Laryngeal paralysis," she said once she had studied the results. "His bark box—his larynx—is paralyzed. Nobody knows what causes it, but it happens, most commonly in racehorses. They call them 'roarers.' I'll give him something for it, a cortisone-based drug called prednisone. Just a five-milligram pill every other day. It can't cure the problem, but at least it'll relieve the inflammation, make it easier for him to swallow."

"Can I hunt him?"

"Sure," she said, tousling Luke's ears as he looked gravely up at her. Jean often rode her own horses near coverts we hunted, along a wild, wooded ridge just back of town. Sometimes she would tell me where she had seen grouse dusting or feeding. She knew what Luke was made of—all heart.

"Bird hunting," she told him now. "That's what you live for, isn't it?"

His ears perked, and his tail thumped: *Yes, indeed!*

But clearly, and sadly, it was time to start looking for a replacement dog. No sooner had I decided to seek a puppy than my friend

Dan Gerber called from Michigan. A fine poet, novelist, and one-time sports car racer—until a 100-mph meeting with a wall at Riverside (California) International Raceway in 1966 convinced him that words were gentler than wheels—Dan had recently endured what I would have to face in a year or two. He had had to put down his dear old dog, Lily, a thirteen-year-old yellow Labrador who had figured powerfully and poignantly in many of his writings.

"I've backtracked Lily's bloodlines," Dan told me, "and located a yellow Lab female who's going to whelp in mid-August. She's the image of Lily—same gentle disposition—and the puppies will be ready for weaning in early October. You want one?"

Dan hadn't hunted Lily as hard as I hunt my dogs, though the few times we had been out with her together she looked keen enough. You certainly couldn't fault her for intelligence and what dog men call biddability—the eagerness to please and learn. And she was one of the gentlest, calmest, most affable dogs I had ever known—saving Luke, certainly.

"Of course," I said.

Done and done. Now all that remained was to drive to Dan's place to collect the pup, a nine-hundred-mile trip from my home in southwestern Vermont to his in western Michigan. I took off bright and early one morning in October, accompanied by a pal, Sean Donovan. By alternating at the wheel of my GMC Jimmy, we would make the trip in one shot, on interstates or high-speed highways almost the entire distance, with plenty of coffee and conversation to keep us rolling.

It devolved into a virtually nonstop monologue about the gundogs in my life to date. Sean, not a bird hunter but a gentleman nonetheless, distinguished himself as a good listener. He heard more than he probably cared to—about Rusty and Belle, the neighborhood Irish setters who had picked me up after school during my boyhood in Wisconsin and led me and my old single-barreled .410 shotgun into virgin woods and fields after prairie chickens, sharp-tailed grouse, woodcock, snipe, Hungarian partridge, ruffed grouse, and big, gaudy ring-necked pheasants (the glamour birds of my youth) that would erupt off the ground, cackling like airborne alarm clocks, when the setters double-teamed them and put an end to their raucous escape plans.

Later, after I had married and moved to New York, there was Peter, my first black Lab, raised from a puppy to hunt the woods and overgrown meadows of Westchester County. But Peter disappeared before his time. Dognappers had been working the area, my wife, Louise, and I learned too late, and I suspect they trolled Peter into a van, using a bitch in heat as bait. Bitter and disconsolate over the loss, I vowed that my next dog would live in a backyard kennel and dog run except when he was out hunting with me.

German shorthaired pointers were all the rage then—the mid-1960s—and Max was a superb specimen. He could cover a twenty-acre meadow like a supersonic vacuum cleaner, lock on point and hold it as solidly as a bridge pier, mark a bird down in the thickest of cover and fetch it back—most of the time—undented by canine teeth. One bleak, windy November afternoon, we flushed a solitary quail out of a stone-wall covert. I fired when it had cleared the tree line, saw it fold and fall. I sent Max to fetch, then followed when he didn't return in his usual ten seconds. I found him sniffing all around for the bird, to no apparent avail. After twenty minutes or so, I called him off and we hunted on. Then, after about an hour, I noticed that Max's cheek was swollen. He must have cut it on some rusty barbed wire, I thought, and called him over to examine it. He was reluctant to come.

"Get over here!" He came in, slinking and avoiding my eyes. "Sit!"

I turned his head to look at the cheek. My God, a growth had sprouted from the corner of his mouth! I looked again and saw . . . the head of a quail, peeking out at me, all covered in saliva.

"Give, Max."

He spit the wounded bird out, then sneaked away shamefacedly. He'd collected the quail I'd knocked down, all right, then kept it hidden in his mouth, sucking it, for more than an hour, savoring it like a feathery jawbreaker.

But good as he was in the field, Max just wasn't a Labrador. A one-man dog, he was surly with visitors, hated kids, and because he had been raised in the kennel and run I built for him and lived most of the time outdoors, was never housebroken—which made for some ugly scenes when I would go soft and invite him inside during subzero weather. So we acquired another Lab—a yellow one this time, eighteen months old when we gladly took him off the hands of a British couple who were moving back to England. His name was Simba (leave it to the Brits to name a dog for a cat) and he was truly leonine in both size—105 pounds, with a head like a pale gold anvil—and dignity.

For a few years, I hunted Max and Simba as a team, pointer and flushing retriever, and was in bird-dog heaven. Max would hunt the overgrown fields and thickets to my right, while Simba coursed the brush-grown stone walls to my left. But Max contracted heartworm, then virtually unknown in the Northeast though endemic in the South. We took him to three vets before one of them diagnosed it. It was too late. He fought, hard and valiantly. Then one foggy spring morning I woke just at dawn and knew he had lost. I went down to where I had bedded him in the kitchen, stared at him for a while, cold there on the linoleum floor. He was only five years old.

I wrapped Max in his blanket for the last time and tried not to cry. With him died my interest in owning pointers. I would be a Labrador man from then on.

Why, you might ask (and many have), would a dedicated upland bird hunter prefer a Lab to the more surefire pointing breeds? Wouldn't a more traditional dog such as an English setter or pointer, a German shorthair or a Brittany spaniel—actually the dog of choice in my part of New England—produce more birds for you? Of course it would, but not the way I like to hunt them. I certainly admire the control and walking-on-eggs caution a good pointing dog exercises in his craft, but I'm not out for a high body count. I much prefer the spontaneity of hunting behind a flushing dog. There's a kind of existential rhythm to pounding along fast behind your dog, seeing him get birdy, tail going like mad, then having him check back to make sure you are ready before he plunges in to flush the bird. It all happens so suddenly. The birds seem to materialize out of nothingness, already moving fast, and are as quickly gone, or dead. You learn to shoot from any position. You may not get as many shots or hit as many birds, but you never lose any wounded ones that might elude a less effective retriever than a Labrador.

And, anyway, I just love Labs. The ones I've known over the years have had a greater sense of fun and retained it longer after puppyhood than any other breed I'm familiar with. I can see many moods in a Labrador's eyes—seriousness, resentment, anticipation, anxiety, sometimes gravity, sometimes even scorn or contempt, but most often love and its jolly twin, playfulness. Am I being anthropomorphic—attributing human emotions to a creature incapable of them? Perhaps, but then, I'm an anthropoid.

I'm not the only Lab fancier to find a nearly human quality in these dogs. In his *Recollections of Labrador Life*, first published in 1861, a traveler named Lambert de Boilieu had this to say of the breed: "The Labrador dog, let me remark, is a bold fellow, and, when well taught, understands, almost as well as any Christian biped, what you say to him."

Where did this paragon of dogdom come from? Zoologists recognize about four hundred breeds of domestic dog (*Canis familiaris*) throughout the world, all of them apparently derived from one of the small, wild subspecies of wolves found in southern Eurasia—perhaps the Indian wolf (*C. lupus pallipes*) or the Chinese wolf (*C. l. chanco*). Fossil finds from places as widely separated as Idaho and Iraq show that the dog was domesticated at least eleven thousand or twelve thousand years ago, while a specimen found more recently in the northern Yukon dates man's best friendship to twenty thousand years' standing. Early humans tamed the dog for many purposes: as a hunting partner, a draft animal, a guardian of camps and later flocks, for war, and even used them as a food source. American Indians ate their dogs during hard times, and dog meat is still a great delicacy in China and other Asian countries. But it's as a hunter that the dog most gladly assists mankind—and in my opinion, none more so than a Lab.

Richard A. Wolters, the foremost American champion of the breed, traces the Lab's origins back to sixteenth-century France, where a breed known as the Saint Hubert's hound was used to track "farre straggled" wounded game—in short, as a retriever. In his 1981 book *The Labrador Retriever: The History . . . The People*, Wolters cites an English text by one George Turberville published in 1576, *The Booke of Hunting*, which lists the types of dogs commonly used in England for hunting, and contains a chapter entitled "Of blacke hounds aunciently come from Sainct Huberts abbay in Ardene." A woodcut accompanying the text shows a lop-eared, strong-tailed, wide-eyed, smooth-coated black dog with the distinctive Labrador head and gaze, even down to the

questioningly furrowed brow peculiar to the breed today—though no Labs I've ever seen look quite as sheeplike as Turberville's hound.

Wolters argues from this evidence that the ancestral Labrador retriever was already common to the West Country lowlands of Devonshire, where men subsisted by waterfowl hunting and fishing. Seamen from Devon, he continues, would logically have brought these superb water dogs with them to the New World when they began fishing the Newfoundland banks in the early sixteenth century, if only to aid them in their fishing and in hunting the abundant game they found ashore.

British sea captains and fishermen in the early 1800s saw black dogs of the Lab's general description being used by commercial fishermen on the Avalon Peninsula around St. John's, Newfound-

Some experts feel that the Saint Hubert's hound of sixteenth-century France could have been the ancestor of today's Labrador retrievers. Note the distinctively quizzical gaze in this woodcut.

land, and recognized their potential as a sporting breed, mainly for retrieving waterfowl shot over their home marshes. The Avalon fishermen, who knew the breed as the "St. John's dog" or the "Newfoundland water dog," took the dogs with them in their dories when they were working longlines. Fish sometimes came off the barbless hooks of the shorter drop lines attached to the longlines as they were pulled into the boat. The "water dogs" would leap overboard on command to fetch the escaping fish. They would also swim out from a dory to pick up net floats and bring them back for hauling. Clearly this aptitude for working in frigid, storm-wild waters could be suited to a sport hunter's benefit.

By 1814, the appellation "Labrador" began to be used for this breed—Labrador being a part of the province of Newfoundland, and certainly its wildest, most game-rich region. In his *Instructions to Young Sportsmen*, published in that year, the British hunting authority Colonel Peter Hawker calls the Labrador dog "by far the best for every kind of shooting . . . Their sense of smelling is scarcely to be credited. Their discrimination of scent, in following a wounded pheasant through a whole covert full of game, or a pinioned wild fowl through a furze brake, or warren of rabbits, appears almost impossible . . . For finding wounded game, of every description, there is not his equal in the canine race; and he is a *sine quâ non* in the general pursuit of wildfowl . . .

"I have tried poodles, but always found them inferior in strength, scent, and courage. They are also very apt to be seasick."

Richard Wolters, in the course of twenty thousand miles and two years spent researching and writing his history of the Labrador retriever, tracked down and visited what he believes to have been the last two surviving representatives of the original "Newfoundland water dog." Unfortunately both were males, then aged thirteen and fifteen, when he located them in the remote fishing village of Grand Bruit, on Newfoundland's bleak south coast.

"He looked much like a Labrador in every way," Wolters wrote of his first meeting with Lassie, the ironically cross-named thirteen-year-old male. "The white on his chest and feet still comes through in some of our Labs today. He was the missing link. His ears were small just like a Lab I used to have. His head was not as square as some of today's show stock but you couldn't miss him for a Lab: as old as he was, he had that brainy look." And despite his age, he remained playful. "Lassie is still very alert," Wolters added, "is an excellent retriever and will come to life just like a puppy when the stick is thrown in the water."

In many respects, the most important quality handed down from the Saint Hubert's hound through the Newfoundland water dog to the Labrador retriever of today is this unquenchable spirit of playfulness. If handled correctly, it can be turned to a dog owner's advantage in training. And dogs must be trained, at least in civil behavior, whether they're to be hunting partners or simply good companions around the house.

Dogs that develop their own games—garbage-can dumping, car chasing, playing at steam shovel in a neighbor's tulip bed, or howl-ing all night at the moon—not only can bring bad blood to a neighborhood (even a remote one, like mine) but can themselves end up dead: under the wheels of a car, by poisoning, or as the result of a neighbor's carefully administered "lead headache," a bullet through the brain.

But by using a dog's desire to play—truly, its *need* to play—to teach it worthwhile "games" such as sitting on command, walking at heel, and hunting and fetching, the dog's owner will keep his canine companion both happy and out of trouble. All dogs, even a tiny terrier or Pekingese, want to have jobs. Any job will do. Once they're shown what it is, what's expected of them, they will perform that function to the best of their ability, with class and style and an unmistakable pride. Unlike humans, however, they don't expect remuneration—only praise for a job well done, or correction if it isn't.

I don't believe anything more than the human voice is needed in correcting a dog's errors. Labs are particularly sensitive to tones of voice, even looks of approval or disapproval. Keep your eyes on your dog whenever you can, and talk to him as you would a person. None of this baby talk—dogs deserve better than that. Don't be surprised if your dog, as he matures, develops at least a listening vocabulary. Words such as "out" and "walk," "supper-time" and "bedtime" should be quickly understood, along with "no" and "good dog." I once calculated that my yellow Lab Simba had a vocabulary in excess of one hundred words. My wife and I had to resort to Spanish or German when debating if and when we were going to take him for a walk/hike/stroll/

jaunt/perambulation/constitutional/promenade/saunter/ramble/
traipse, or stretch of the legs. Even at that, it took him only a week
to equate *paseo* and *Spaziergang* with all of the above.

"I think I'll remove the *perro amarillo* from the premises for a
brief *paseo* before retiring."

Arf, arf, whine, whine—and a whirlwind dash toward the back
door.

Luke, on the other hand, could read my mind, I swear. I'd be
sitting upstairs at the typewriter in my office, with a few hundred
words painfully pecked out, when my thoughts would stray to the
bird covers: which ones should we hunt today? Better give the
ridge a rest—we hit it pretty hard yesterday. Maybe Dorset Mountain? No, it's Saturday—could be flatlanders in there. How about
the Woodcock Islands up the road; we haven't been there in a
while, and flight birds may have arrived.

Heavy breathing from the foot of the stairs, followed by a ten-
tative moan. Then the slow clump of footsteps up the stairway.
Luke's head peeks around the corner of the banister. His eyes lock
on mine, then shift to the gun cabinet across from my desk. His
eyes hold the question. Mine answer, involuntarily . . . And he's
dancing on the carpet, lit up like a hunk of anthracite, his eyes
sparking with joy. Drumming up enthusiasm.

I could say "No!" and he'd slink away to mumble and mutter
downstairs, doggy curses at the unfairness of it all, the birds *are*
there, he knows it from the weather, from the cocky tang in the
air, the hum of the planets, the stare of the moon last night. How
can I deny him? I take down the shotgun and reach for my
boots . . .

Luke's job and mine are one: together we kill game birds. Nothing else matters: not sex or food or comfort, not sleep or warmth,
water or love. We're not merely a "team," man and dog, but a
single being with a single-minded mission: to pound the hills for-
ever, through briers and cold and muck and barbed wire, putting
birds up in a roar of wings and knocking them down again with
a bang and reek of gunpowder, fetching back the warm bird and
stuffing it into a cold game pocket, stained black with bird blood
these many years. Later we eat them. (Yes, I always give Luke a
few table scraps, especially when we eat game birds.)

At moments like this, Luke is all business, and so am I. We're driven by the same gods or demons: the wolf is revealed in all his cruel glory. Without Luke I'd be a dilettante. With him I'm a hunter. We transcend ourselves—he's more than a dog, I'm more than a man. Hunting alone, I would leave most of these birds unharmed, unseen perhaps, certainly unflighted. Left to his own devices, he would fly them, all right, but they'd never fall. Together we both fly them and fell them, interrupt the arc, break the rainbow, prove the Second Law of Thermodynamics and yet disprove it at the same time. These birds we kill fly on in my dreams, and in Luke's dreams, too. In sleep, our legs twitch in synchrony, old muscles now, bone-stiff and bone-weary. Blood crusts on his thorn-ripped nose, blood scabs on my thorn-ripped hands.

Yes, I love Labs for their playfulness.

Sean and I had arrived at Dan's lakeside home north of Fremont, Michigan, at midnight, then drove the forty-odd miles south to Zeeland the next morning in Dan's Range Rover to collect the pups. The breeders, a gracious couple named Grace and Myron Morris, had asked Dan and me to choose names for the pups soon after they were born, so that by the time we picked them up eight weeks later, they would respond when called. They did.

Jake wasn't much to look at when he was born—more like a drowned rat than a Labrador pup.

At first glance, the puppy waddling toward me that day, grinning and flailing his short, thick tail so violently that it threatened to wag him off his feet, was as lovable as they come—but he looked more like a furry piglet or a blond bear cub than a registered, blue-blooded Labrador retriever with the high-flown name of Toynton's Kent Hollow Jake. His sister, whom Dan Gerber had dubbed

But by the time I met Jake at the age of eight weeks, he already had a vivacious personality and a friendly, lovable smile.

Toynton's Willa (after Willa Cather), looked just the same. "They're clever little rascals," Grace Morris said. "Real quick to learn."

With the pups at our heels, we went down to the big kennels behind the Morris house to have a look at Jake and Willa's sire, Shamrock Acres Reign Maker, more familiarly known as Dewey. He proved to be a massive, friendly yellow Lab with wide-set eyes in a large head. "He weighs a hundred pounds," Grace said, "with not a speck of fat on him." The pups' dam, Millie (more formally, Toynton's Millicent After Six), was smaller, of course, but similarly equable in disposition. She was a bit brusque with the pups, though, when they dived at her still-sagging and red-chawed dugs

He got a goodbye kiss from his mother, Millie, or perhaps it was just a final face wash.

Grace Morris, the Michigan breeder who saw Jake through his first weeks of life, received a moist farewell lick.

for a now illicit snack. "There were only three puppies in the litter," Grace told us, "two male and one female. The other male, Hogan, left yesterday with his owners." Sean, who had perked up at the news that there was a third pup in the litter, looked a bit downcast. Later he told me, "If I'd known how great they were, I'd have put in with you for one of them."

Grace had baked some bread and chocolate chip cookies, so over coffee and snacks in her kitchen, with the pups fussing at our feet, we listened to feeding, health, and training suggestions. "I'd appreciate it if you'd keep in touch," Grace said. "Send me a note on their progress and a picture now and then. These dogs will mean a lot to you, I know, but they mean a lot to me, too."

"Come on," Dan said to me, grinning. "Let's get home and roll around on the floor and chew on our puppies."

We did just that, then took Jake and Willa for a long walk through the beech woods surrounding Dan's house. The pups staggered, flopped, stumbled over twigs, ambushed each other, splashed joyfully through every mud puddle along the way, and in general fulfilled all the puppy clichés, but they kept up. At one point a ruffed grouse blew out of a downed pine tree about fifty

Dan Gerber and I took Jake and his sister, Willa, for a long, rambling walk through the woods.

yards ahead of us. They looked up at the roar of the bird's wings, but clearly their eyes couldn't focus that far ahead yet.

"They'll see better in time," I said.

Dan nodded, then got down on his knees in the mud and regarded the pups. "I would like to compliment both of you," he told them solemnly. "Your puppy disguises are perfect. You have every last mannerism down to a T. I believe you're fully prepared now for your secret mission."

The pups waggled their outsized heads joyfully, then Willa leaped on Jake and knocked him flat in a mud puddle.

The pair of them slept well that night, their last together for quite a while. Grace had warned us that the pups woke up at 5:30 a.m. sharp, "regular as an alarm clock," and early the next morning—after a hearty breakfast of puppy chow (for Jake) and a quick perambulation in the woods—Sean and I bundled Jake into the travel kennel in the back of my Jimmy and headed east. The pup surprised us by not fussing a bit on separation from the last of his littermates. With occasional pit stops for feeding and piddle breaks, the return trip was painless for all hands.

Louise and our menagerie—Luke plus three cats, one a four-month-old kitten—were waiting when I wheeled into the barnyard early the next day. Jake was the object of all eyes and noses. Louise oohed and aahed and cuddled. Luke sniffed the pup from stem to stern, wagged his tail halfheartedly, yawned, then walked off: What else is new? The two older cats, Sam and Ninja, took one look at the newcomer, hissed in loud feline horror, and headed for the hills, where they remained for the better part of the next two weeks.

The kitten, Spike Jones, welcomed Jake like a long-lost brother. Louise, as much a sucker for baby animals as I, had acquired Spike in August while I was fishing for brook trout in Canada. He had been received coolly, to say the least, by the adult pets. Luke, always easygoing, allowed Spike a few liberties, such as letting the kitten cuddle against him while both of them snoozed, but when Spike tried to play floor hockey with the tip of Luke's tail, he growled ominously. Sam eventually permitted the kitten to walk within easy striking range, even brush against him, though if Spike essayed a little kittenish roughhouse—for example, quick, claw-sheathed left jabs at Sam's beezer—the old neutered tom merely

slammed the kitten to the floor and stalked disdainfully away. Ninja, who brooks no familiarities from anyone of any species or any size, slapped the kitten silly the first time she realized that Spike was living with us permanently, and every time thereafter if he so much as walked into the same room with her. The message was clear, and Spike heeded it. And heeds it to this day, though he's twice Ninja's size.

As soon as Jake entered the household, however, he and Spike were playmates and pals, young drawn to young, and about the same length, though Jake, of course, was taller and heavier. They raced at each other, embraced on their hind legs, and immediately began mouth wrestling. The clumsy yellow puppy and the agile black-and-white kitten zoomed around the house in a piebald blur.

Back at my home in Vermont, the new arrival seemed happy to meet Luke, who would be his mentor in the year to come.

Jake loved nothing more than to take Spike's head in his mouth
and seemingly—to our initial horror—gnaw on it like a soupbone.
Or he would grab Spike by a hind paw, chew his toenails, then
drag the kitten around for a while.

Conversely, when Jake flopped down for one of his instant,
quarter-hourly naps, Spike would stalk him as a lion might a buf-
falo, then spring on the pup in mid-snore, deliver a dozen snake-
quick blows to the head, and split for cover before Jake knew what
had happened. Spike's preferred hideouts were under the coffee
table and beneath the skirted hassock of my favorite living room
chair. There he would lurk until Jake clumped by, at which point

Jake found a playful pal in our kitten, Spike Jones.

a razor-tipped paw would dart out and zap Jake's hocks. While Jake tried to snuffle into the hideaway, the kitten would escape out the other side. The game would be repeated ad infinitum, much to the discomposure of the rest of the household. You never knew when a kitten-and-puppy bullet train might whiz between your legs.

On trips into town, I made it a point to take Jake with me. That way, I reasoned, his easygoing familiarity with motor travel, well learned on the long drive back from Michigan, would remain intact. One of Luke's few drawbacks was that whenever I took him with me in the truck, he reckoned we were heading for a grouse cover, so he would get "up" for it—yelping, shivering, now and then breaking into a querulous, barely controlled yowl that threatened to rupture my eardrums. I once took him on what should have been the bird-hunting trip of a lifetime—an expedition to New Brunswick after woodcock. New Brunswick is the major breeding ground for most of the woodcock that migrate down the Atlantic coast each autumn: a wellspring of Luke's favorite game bird that overflows at the first hard frost of the year to send thousands of woodcock south for the winter. Catching these flight birds just as they're congregating and beginning to move out in small clusters is every Eastern upland hunter's dream, and his dog's, too, unless I miss my guess.

But it's a thirteen- or fourteen-hour drive from my place to Sackville, New Brunswick, where we were to meet the men we were hunting with: writers Charles Gaines and P. J. O'Rourke, and Geoff Thomas, a New Zealand trout guide I'd fished with years earlier. It was half a day of sheer motorized hell, with Luke yipping and fidgeting all the way, moaning to himself, and no doubt cursing me for not driving faster. If you think children are troublesome on a long car trip—"Daddy, are we there yet?"—try a journey with an overeager Lab sometime. Even worse, when we finally reached the hotel in Sackville that would be our base camp for the daily bird hunts (an establishment, by the way, that welcomes into its elegant rooms bird dogs as well as "bird-hunting gentlemen"), Luke refused the hospitality. He preferred the back seat of the van. That way, I suppose, he could imagine that I'd be out and driving to the nearest cover any minute now. He was so supercharged with anticipation that by the time we finally got into the woods, he forgot all the caution learned over eight years of hunting and reverted to his puppyhood habits of charging far out ahead of the guns after every stray bird scent. He finally did settle down, though, and we got in some splendid shooting.

On another occasion, Charles Gaines and an associate, Chris Child, came over to Vermont to hunt with us. I made the mistake of keeping Luke in the truck while we hunted Charles's Brittany spaniel, Tucker, on the first swing of the day through one of my favorite upland covers. It was a warm morning, so I'd left the windows of the truck open an inch or two to give Luke some air while he waited. Unfortunately, Tucker went on point only fifty yards from the truck. Charles went in ahead of Tucker's point to flush the bird—a grouse—and shot as it rose. The bird fell, near a stone wall overgrown with briers, and the next thing I knew, Luke was darting in to retrieve it. For a moment I thought nothing of the fact, it was such a familiar sight by now—Luke making another nose-perfect retrieve. But then . . . hey, he's supposed to be locked in the truck! He brought the bird in and I noticed blood on his mouth. It wasn't grouse blood. I ran back to the truck and saw that, at the shot, Luke had crashed through the driver's-side truck window, through sheer shatterproof glass, like a seventy-pound black boulder. Luckily, the glass had only cut his lip slightly and no harm was done. Gaines and Child were mightily impressed with Luke's determination. He hunted with us, honoring Tucker's points, for the rest of the day.

No, I certainly couldn't fault Luke for eagerness, but it was a bit embarrassing—especially when the neighbors half a mile down the road told me they could always tell by the accompanying sound effects when I was heading for a distant bird cover in the truck.

Jake stayed calm on our drives, though, and I discovered another unsuspected benefit to taking your puppy with you while running errands: good-looking women, who wouldn't have looked twice at an old geezer by his lonesome, now stopped to coo over the puppy. "He's just *adorable*!" they would say, then gaze up at me with soft, loving eyes. I rather bashfully reported this phenomenon to my wife. "What do you expect?" She said, wryly. "Good-looking guys say the same thing to me!"

Jake was puzzled when strangers stopped to smile and coo over him, though he certainly enjoyed the attention.

So young Jake was accommodating very nicely to our domestic situation. It remained to be seen, though, how well he would adapt to his primary role as gundog and heir to the exemplary Luke. I couldn't expect Jake to develop into a finished hunting dog in just one season, certainly not with him starting this young in life. All of my earlier dogs had been born in the spring, so that by the time they first went afield with me in the fall, they were at least five months old. I had never started a puppy this young before, but I knew that I could determine if he had the makings, anyway. And I hoped that just by tagging along in company with Luke, he might get a glimmer of what it was all about.

The first step in the pup's education was to get him used to gunfire. The day after Sean and I arrived back from Michigan with Jake, Sean and his seven-year-old son, Richard, came over to help me. While Richard held Jake on a leash about thirty feet away, Sean threw clay pigeons for me from a foot trap. I popped them with a 20-gauge. Not only did Jake not flinch or seem frightened in the least by the noise, he appeared positively overjoyed by it. Richard brought him closer as I shot six clay birds in a row, and at the

But he was also ready for more serious business— learning the gun dog's trade.

end he was sitting directly under the muzzle of the gun. A good start. And when we finally let Jake loose, he waddled straight out into the field and brought back a shattered clay pigeon—his first retrieve.

That afternoon I took Jake with me while Luke and I hunted the cover behind my house. It was sunny and brisk, with a light northwest wind, and a frost the previous night had the maple leaves falling like giant golden snowflakes. Jake trotted along right at my heels, his brand-new collar bell jangling, while Luke quartered ahead of us, staying within shooting range. About a half mile up

Training Jake to the sound of shotgun fire while blasting clay pigeons, I found him fearless and eager. Then he even retrieved one of the less damaged clays—to chew it.

Luke led the way on Jake's first hunts, teaching the pup how to find what we were seeking—game birds. When Luke flushed, then retrieved a woodcock, Jake grasped the lesson.

the woods road, Luke flushed a woodcock that flew out straight down the trail—a lead-pipe-cinch shot, which I missed. With both barrels. I would like to say I was distracted by the puppy's being underfoot, but it was just plain lousy shooting. Still, Jake seemed to see the bird get up and intently watched it fly away, at least as far as he could focus. After that, Jake tried to run with Luke as the older dog quartered for birds, but he was still too small to keep up unless Luke purposely slowed down for him.

We flushed two more birds—grouse—on the way back in, but saw neither of them in the thick cover, so I didn't shoot. All told, we were out an hour and a quarter, and Jake seemed ready for a nap. I left him at home while Luke and I went to another cover, where I killed two woodcock. When we got home, just before dark, Jake was awake. I let him sniff one of the dead birds. He stared at it for a moment, then glommed it with a growl. Later, I let him worry one of the wings while I cleaned the birds, so he could get the taste of it. He mouthed it quite gently, with the inborn caution of any baby confronting something new, and I reinforced him with encouraging words. When he got bolder and started to chomp down on the wing, I distracted him and "dis-

Then Jake dashed ahead over every obstacle to find birds on his own.

Sometimes the going got rough for the puppy, through muddy swales and over wind-felled trees, but young Jake charged on.

appeared" it, then quickly got him into the house, where Spike was waiting to distract him further.

In my gunning diary for that day, I wrote: *Jake's first day afield. Not gun-shy, not afraid of the woods, ready to run with Luke when Luke will let him. Doesn't dislike the smell or taste of woodcock— indeed, he's keen for them. Didn't whine or sulk when I inadvertently clipped his jaw as he followed on my heels. Motored over and under logs & through mud & streams quite manfully—as if it were old stuff for him. Came when I called or whistled to him. All told, looks quite hopeful.*

He proved to be a quick study on other counts as well. House-breaking came easily to him: at night, and for his frequent naps, we'd put him in his portable kennel in the dining room, where he'd quickly curl up on a blanket. Since a dog—even a puppy—

will not foul its own den, it was an easy matter to whisk him outside when he woke up, and he soon learned that that was the place to do his "business."

Teaching Jake to walk at heel took a bit more time. A puppy's instinct is to dash ahead, investigating things that pique its curiosity—though not too far, since most young animals have an innate sense of caution and usually stay within easy rescue range of the "parent" to whom they're bonded. With Jake on a leash, I'd position him at my side, the handle of the leash in one hand,

Training Jake to walk at heel, I used a light leash at first. But soon he learned to stay at my side on command, running ahead only when I gestured him to go.

but with the other loosely grasping the slack. (I wanted him to heel close enough so that he wasn't walking "under the gun.") I'd repeat the command "Heel!" every few steps at first, reinforcing the order with a light, sharp pull on the slack loop in my hand. Whenever Jake tried to dash ahead, I'd give him another light pull and say, "Whoa, Jake! Heel!" And when he did so: "Good boy, Jake!"

In short order, he was responding. I lengthened the time between repetitions of the "Heel!" command, reduced the strength of the pulls on the slack loop to the merest pressure, and after a few weeks of lessons—perhaps five or six a day, on walks to the barn, to and from the mailbox, or down the dirt road we live on—I removed the leash entirely. "Whoa!" and "Heel!" were now sufficient to keep him just where I wanted him. When I wanted him to range ahead, I'd say "Jake, go ahead!" and accompany the command with an underhand casting motion in the direction I wished him to take.

Teaching him decorum indoors was fairly easy. He wanted to

He learned "Sit!" and "Stay!"
just as readily—all of which
was mere basic training for
his primary mission:
retrieving.

be near me most of the time, so when I was sitting down I'd occasionally let one hand dangle near the floor. He'd rub and nuzzle against it and I'd fondle his head, let him chew on my hand—but say "No!" quite firmly when he bit down too hard. That way he not only learned "No!" and how to moderate the strength of his bite but grew familiar with my hand on his muzzle. Whenever he barked out of turn, I'd quickly clamp his jaw shut and order, "Quiet, Jake! Stop that noise!" I didn't want him to stop barking entirely while he was inside: I value a dog's sharp ears that can hear things beyond our range, and his barking at strange noises serves as a warning of approaching visitors or, God forbid, burglars. Old Luke had long since learned to distinguish the sound of my wife's car engine as it came up the hill, bringing her home from work, and would dash to the back door all a-wag and barking with delight while she was still half a mile or more away. Jake quickly learned the engine's sound as well, and I allowed him to bark along with Luke—we're all happy when she gets home.

Though both dogs were amply fed twice a day, morning and evening, I occasionally gave them Milk-Bone dog biscuits as snacks, mainly to let them know I was the fount of all their delights (thus reinforcing the bond between us), but sometimes as a reward for being "good boys." It sounds kind of patronizing, but dogs don't seem to resent it a bit. "Cookie time!" was the magic phrase. Luke, of course, would immediately trot over to the blue spice cabinet in the kitchen where the Milk-Bones lived and sit alertly, ears cocked, watching my every move. Jake soon followed suit—doggie see, doggie do—and I reinforced the "Sit!" command by pointing skyward with the index finger of one upraised hand. When they were sitting side by side, watching me, I'd take two biscuits from

the box. "Luke first," I'd say, then give Luke his "cookie." He always took it politely and gently. If Jake, with his puppy voracity, tried to grab Luke's biscuit from my hand, I'd lower and harshen my voice: "No, Jake!" and then offer him his biscuit when he'd resumed his position. If he snapped at it in his eagerness, I'd lift it out of reach. "Nicely, now, Jake!" I'd say. Soon he was taking the dog biscuit from my fingers as gently as Luke did. I'd learned long ago, with earlier dogs, that wolfish snapping after proffered snacks can be harmful to hand health. Moreover, this training taught the puppy more about the potential strength of his jaws, and the need to control them. Learning to use them gently would be of value in the field. A hard-mouthed dog that maims and mangles the birds he retrieves is almost as bad as no dog at all.

I spent plenty of time outdoors with Jake, reinforcing his instinct to fetch by tossing a canvas-covered retrieving "bumper" for him. He learned to sit on command—one blast on the Acme-Thunderer police whistle combined with a forefinger held upright while maintaining firm eye contact with him. He learned to stay—the palm of the hand held upright, toward him, with eye contact still maintained—until the bumper hit the ground. Then I'd deliver the command "Fetch!" accompanied by an underhand casting motion of my arm in the direction of the bumper, and he'd line

The canvas-covered "bumper" soon was Jake's favorite toy. From "Sit!" and "Stay!" he graduated to "Fetch!" It's a game we play every day, even now that he's grown.

out for it. As soon as he had it in his jaws, I'd blow twice on the whistle and motion him back to me. Each retrieve won him warm praise: "Good boy, Jake! Attaway to do it! You're a good dog, Jake!" And a few rough pats on the head, or scratchings at the root of his tail—a puppy can't get enough praise or petting when he does well.

The moment he lost concentration during those early lessons—distracted, perhaps, by a passing butterfly, or the arrival of another person or animal on the scene—I'd stop the retrieving session. Ten or twenty minutes was usually enough, anyway. A puppy's attention span is no great shakes. Twenty minutes of "work" was enough to make him ready for another nap, and into his kennel he'd go.

When Jake wasn't sleeping or learning whistle signals and retrieving, he'd follow me around the property. He was awed by the woodpile, studying it gravely as I threw logs into the cart and brought them into the house or fed them to the wood stove. He was fascinated by the pansies that grew in two half barrels near the back stoop, initially attracted by the buzz of feeding bees, I think, but then by the flowers themselves, especially when my wife

or I would dead-head them, pinching off withered blossoms to encourage new growth. I let him chew on a few of these dead heads, but when he started biting off flowers on his own it was time for a firm "No!" and a quick removal to another part of the yard. Puppies are easily diverted—everything is new and wonderful to them. It all has to be sniffed, mouthed, chewed, batted around, or splashed in. The vegetable garden was a source of marvels: windfall tomatoes knocked down and spoiled by a sudden storm (but too tart, he learned, for prolonged chewing), a worm-channeled ear of overripe sweet corn (much more rewarding than tomatoes), leathery string beans missed in the harvest—all the detritus of an over-the-hill kitchen garden awaiting its fall cleanup. The brook that ran through the bottom of the yard was even more fun. Not only could Jake splash through it most spectacularly,

But all work and no play might make Jake a dull boy. He amused himself with found objects: a padded tea cozy, a multitude of twigs, or even the leg of a plastic lawn table.

throwing great loud geysers into the air, but now and then strange, swift, speckled creatures would dart away from the sides of sub-merged boulders—brook trout too fast for him to catch, though he tried.

In the yard, and in the fifteen acres of meadow that surrounded it, there were songbirds to flush, robins and blackbirds and mea-dowlarks. Whenever he'd make one fly, I'd whistle him to sit, then call him to me and praise him. At dusk, when Luke was snoozing inside, Jake and I would sit together on the back stoop and watch bats hawking for moths in the twilight. His eyes would follow them solemnly, then look over to me. I'd nod to him with equal gravity. "They're not for us, Jakey. A waste of ammunition. We can't eat 'em, and, besides, they clean up a lot of mosquitoes." He'd yawn and stretch. Bedtime.

• • •

But Jake's most important lessons came in the game bird covers, under a far better teacher than I could ever hope to be—the Maestro of the Uplands, Black Luke.

Though men and dogs have been hunting and living together now for thousands of years, no one really knows how a dog perceives the world, or how he puts together the flood of perceptions available to him in the hunting field to find the game he and his clumsy, bipedal partner are seeking. Some of the clues are obvious even to humans: the skittering of bird claws in dry autumn leaves as a grouse legs it away from the approaching hunters; the sign of fresh woodcock droppings, like splatters of whitewash from an overloaded brush, indicating that migrating "flight birds" have at last alighted into a customary but long-empty fall cover. The subtler signs are beyond us. I read somewhere that a good gundog can distinguish some ten thousand different odors, though how this figure was arrived at I do not know—did some researcher dissect a dead dog's nose and trace each nerve end to a particular receptor in its brain? Yet I can believe that statistic, if only from experience. What would seem to me to be fresh grouse tracks in the mud sometimes don't turn Luke on at all, and when I've taken him with me after them into a nearby cover, we never put up a bird.

Jake seemed fascinated with our garden, and even when he got older would now and then pick himself a few flowers or munch on an ear of sweet corn that was past its prime.

At other times he gets birdy, though there's nothing to indicate the presence of grouse or woodcock to me. Once he got excited in the middle of an open field we were crossing, a field of sparse, ankle-high grass that you wouldn't think could hold a cowering titmouse, much less a grouse. And anyway, the wisdom of the ages says grouse are never found in the open.

"Come on, don't be silly," I told him. "Let's get going."

He took four or five quick steps, nose to the ground, and stopped short as a grouse took off. It was as if he'd conjured it up out of thin air. I was so surprised that I missed the shot. Luke looked at me sadly, a portrait of reproach.

"Gone away, boy."

Yeah, sure.

I've finally learned after all these years to believe him when his behavior says "Birds!" But it took him a few seasons to hone those perceptions to what they became, and I hoped he could teach Jake the secrets beyond my ken.

We hunted nearly every day that season, at least two hours and sometimes as many as six, in one or another of the eight covers I've found most productive over the years. Some of these covers, like the one I call Hay Ridge, are vast—two miles long and a mile wide of old white pines and young aspens, alder-grown seeps and ridges spiky with thorn apples, areas of old maples festooned with fox grapes, weathered outcrops of granite and grass studded with hardhack, old fallen-down stone walls, and "volunteer" apple trees which, when they're producing, always attract grouse, and stands of beech or shagbark hickory that do the same. Other covers are best described as "postage stamps." There's a quick look-in spot a few miles up the road from my place that I call the Woodcock Islands. Dotted about a ten-acre meadow that is mowed every summer there are three half-acre stands of aspen, and the meadow itself is rimmed by mixed aspens, pines, and maples. I can hunt each of the aspen islands in perhaps five minutes, or hunt them and the field edge in no more than forty-five minutes. Another cover along a nameless brook, among clumps of old apple trees, takes half an hour.

As Jake's legs strengthened and his attention span grew, I lengthened the hunts and showed him—or I should say Luke showed him—the "hot spots" in each cover, from small to large. At first he just trotted along at Luke's heels, but as he saw Luke get birdy, light up, and begin hunting keenly, nose to the ground, in rapid, tail-flailing arcs and circles, looking for the source of the bird scent,

We hunted practically every day that first season, with Jake growing stronger and more confident mile by mile as we pounded through the bird covers.

On hot days, Luke led Jake to water for a welcome drink—and a mud bath.

Jake began to emulate the older dog. He knew what we were seeking: that explosive rattle of feathers as a bird got up and took the good smell with him. And, watching Luke retrieve or following along after him as he did so, he learned that—yes—sometimes the bird smell returned to earth, following the bang of the shotgun, and its source could indeed be picked up in a dog's mouth. And brought back to the man. Just like a retrieving bumper!

Most hunting dogs will run ahead of a gunner in zigzag patterns, called quartering, searching for scent in a wider area than could be covered if the dog merely trotted straight ahead of the hunter. At first Jake followed Luke's tracks as he quartered through the covers. But Luke stopped one day and looked hard at the puppy. He growled low in his throat, as he did when the ever-hungry Jake tried to encroach on his food bowl at suppertime. Jake came back toward me, crestfallen, but then suddenly an idea seemed to hit him. He began quartering a pattern of his own, exactly parallel to Luke's but about twenty yards to Luke's left. This was just what I'd hoped for—just what Max and Simba used to do.

Whenever the dogs got too far ahead, on the edge of gunshot range, I'd call them in with two blasts of the police whistle. When they were back within range, one whistle blast would make them sit. Then I could signal them to hunt in the direction I wanted to go. Luke was a past master at reading hand signals. If I wanted him to hunt to the right or left of our line, I'd wave that way when I had his attention and he'd go. It took Jake a while to see what was happening, but soon he got the idea—much quicker than it had taken Luke, in his puppy days, to learn it from me. Clearly, this method was a shortcut to teaching a new dog good field behavior. By imitating an older, already trained dog he soon learned what we all wanted, and was rewarded with praise for doing so.

Jake learned other, subtler things from Luke as well. Luke knew where all the sources of water were in the different covers we hunted. Indeed, he had shown them to me in most cases: little brush-hidden rills I'd never have found on my own, secret ponds and springs and seeps that provided a welcome drink on hot, early-season afternoons. Luke knew somehow that in cold weather, grouse would be found in those covers on sunny slopes, out of the wind, and he taught that to Jake as well, just as he'd taught it to me.

Once we were caught in a sudden early-November thunderstorm, and I saw Jake look startled, almost frightened by the first big rumblings from the sky. Before I could reassure him that there was nothing to be afraid of, Luke had run up to him and bumped him with his shoulder, as if to say, "Come on, kid, let's get on with it!" They both tore into a cover on the way back to the truck. We hunted through rain, sleet, or snow, but Luke knew already that when the sky spat fire, we headed for home. Jake learned it that day. A steel-barreled shotgun makes an excellent lightning rod.

Most puppies, in their eagerness to hunt, will chase rabbits, deer, even songbirds the first few times they go afield with their master. The trick is to teach them which game you're hunting and which should be beneath their concern. Even the exemplary Luke had chased a few rabbits and deer during his first couple of seasons—but never very far, always returning to the whistle. And he loved to flush songbirds. Once, when he was two years old, Louise and I were hiking with him along a trail that ran high on Bear Mountain, directly behind our Vermont home, with Luke quartering ahead of us. It was late summer, not yet the hunting season, but fall warblers were already beginning to bunch up for the southward migration. Suddenly we saw Luke get birdy and dart into the heavily leafed brush beside the trail. I called him back and he came proudly, to drop a very outraged, saliva-covered pine warbler at our feet. He must have grabbed it out of the air as it flushed—that's how quick and keen-sighted he was. But he soon lost his interest in non-game birds, focusing his whole heart and soul on grouse, woodcock, and occasional ducks. He also gave up chasing furred game, and I think I know why.

Shortly after we moved to Vermont in 1979, I was hunting him in the covers behind the house when, late one afternoon, he disappeared into a thicket to check it for grouse. The leaves were still dense and I couldn't see him, though he was no more than fifty yards from me. There came a deep, woofing growl, too deep for Luke to have uttered it. He came pelting out of the thicket and skidded to halt at my feet, looking back toward the cover with the whites of his eyes showing. I calmed him and waited a few minutes; then we went back into the thicket. Once my eyes adjusted to the low light in there, I searched the ground for tracks—and found them. Luke had surprised a wandering black bear, one that had just enjoyed a meal of wild blackberries, judging from its droppings. And the bear had surprised Luke as well, enough so that from then on he rarely chased furred game again. The lesson was reinforced later that fall when, on a pitch-black night, after I'd just let him out for a last walk before bedtime, he ran into a skunk. I don't know if he attacked it or it attacked him, but he returned from the dark with his eyes bloodshot and streaming and his head and neck soaked with skunk sap. He did not at all relish being smeared with the number 10 cans of tomatoes—two of them—that it took to neutralize the resultant reek.

In the course of our hunts that first fall, Jake, too, met a lot of extraneous wildlife: woodchucks, a weasel, a flock of wild turkeys, a pileated woodpecker whose loud, machine-gun-like pecking on a dead tree bole caused him to cock his head curiously, a number of rabbits, of course, and many, many deer. But because Luke didn't chase them, Jake didn't either, though he was sorely tempted. I don't know if they encountered any skunks or, potentially worse, porcupines when they were hunting together. But Jake managed to do that on his own, without Luke to offer advice. One afternoon, back at home, I was out working on the woodpile. Luke was snoozing under a pine tree next to the house and Jake was prowling in the newly mowed meadow near the woodpile. My back was turned, but I spun around when I heard Jake go woof. Kee-rist! There he was not a hundred yards from me, dancing lightly around a skunk. The skunk was trying to get its business end aimed at Jake, its back legs hopping back and forth jerkily, and Jake was barking and dodging from side to side. Finally the skunk risked a snap shot—I could see the yellowish musk spray out from its scent glands like the fog from a low-flying crop duster. Jake avoided the main spray, but when the fog hit him he beat a quick retreat. The skunk sauntered off: all in a day's work. Jake endured a tomato bath. But I fear the skunking wasn't severe enough to have taught him a truly memorable lesson.

His run-in with his first—and I hope last—porcupine was memorable, however. I was away from home at the time, but Louise told me about it over the telephone. "I'd let him out last night for a final piddle before I went to bed," she said, "and he ran up in the field. Suddenly I heard him bark. I tried to whistle for him, but it was too late. He barked once more and then let out a yelp. I called him again, and he came sidling in from the dark, into the edge of the back-porch light. God, Bob, he looked like an old sea captain, you know, with those chin whiskers they used to wear? Porcupine bristles—must have been forty or fifty of them. Our own Captain Ahab.'' Louise had to take him to Jean Ceglowski's at eleven o'clock at night to remove the quills under a local anesthetic. I only hope the experience was traumatic enough for him to associate porcupine scent with bad news from now on.

So Jake still hadn't put it all together, but he was getting the gist of it. He knew already that when I pulled on my boots and shooting vest, we were getting ready for something special. He knew that when I buckled on his bell collar—the one that went *clang, clang, clang* when he was wearing it—the moment was near. And he knew that when I brought the shotgun down from the gun cabinet, the moment was indeed right now. In his brief life, that was approximately doggy heaven.

It was on our seventeenth day afield together that Jake flushed his first game bird. I'll never forget that overcast, rather muggy day, with Luke ranging ahead and the woodcock suddenly erupting under Jake's inquisitive nose, with me bringing the gun to my shoulder and centering the bird as it dodged away at speed, yet still aware in my peripheral vision of Jake's eyes locked onto it as it flew, hitting the trigger and seeing the bird puff and fall and bounce on the leaf-strewn ground—and Jake quivering for an instant, then lining out as fast as his puppy legs would carry him toward the fallen prey.

But as my diary records, Luke got there first and asserted his rights as Number-One Dog—still. He made it clear to us both that a dog had his dignity, even if his day was fast waning. Jake honored that right (what other choice did he have?), and I honored it as well, allowing Luke the retrieve on all the birds we killed together through the remainder of that season, no matter which dog had flushed it. Some of the retrieves were tough, and I hoped that by keeping the pup back with me as we watched Luke make them, Jake would learn something. One bird fell in what seemed an impossible tangle of multiflora rose briers that had grown up amid a jungle of aspen tops left behind by loggers. Luke hadn't seen the bird fall—he was off to the side as it flushed over his head—and had to respond to my hand signals to find the spot. When he figured out where I was sending him, he looked up at me as if to say, "You want me to go in *there*?" Then a fluke of the breeze brought him the scent of the downed bird. His ears perked and his tail went up. He circled uphill, looking for a way into the tangle, then walked out along a downed aspen, balancing like an aerialist, until he was directly over the bird. He dove into the thorns, to emerge a minute later with bloody ears and tail—and the bird between his jaws. He dropped the grouse at my feet and looked up, grinning. That's what it's all about.

The pup sat at my feet, staring up at Luke with a quizzical look. Then he looked down at the fallen grouse. A flash of understanding seemed to light his eyes. Oh, I get it. If it flies, it dies. And if it dies, it *fries!*

Perhaps that's a bit farfetched, but I'm amazed at how much Jake learned from Luke during his puppy season. The following summer, fully seven months since the close of his first hunting season, I wanted to see how much he remembered, so I took him alone up to one of my favorite bird covers. It was a hot, humid July day with the worst of scenting conditions, the alders and aspens in full leaf. I clipped on his hunting bell so that I could at least hear where he was working when he was hidden in deep cover, and we pushed into the thicket. He stayed close to me at first but then seemed to recognize the country, moving out from underfoot to quarter ahead of me well within range, though of course I wasn't carrying a shotgun—the 1990 hunting season was still eight weeks in the future. In half an hour he flushed three woodcock and two ruffed grouse, all from within fifteen yards of me judging by the sound of their takeoffs—feathery, heart-stopping explosions in the case of the grouse, quick whistles of wingtips from the smaller, closer-holding woodcock. In that thick greenery I caught only glimpses of the birds themselves. Jake took off after the first of the grouse but came in quickly to two blasts from the Acme-Thunderer.

At the far end of the cover, where the woods thinned, we pushed uphill through spiky thorn apples, across fallen stone walls, to a ridge where I knew there'd be a breeze to cool me off, and a small spring-fed stock pond for Jake. We both needed it. I was pouring sweat and Jake was huffing like the Little Engine That Could. But he wasn't so little anymore—during the winter he'd grown to equal Luke in size, and clearly he'd top out much bigger, perhaps a full head taller and eighty-five pounds to the older dog's seventy.

The pond lay just over the crest of the ridge and Jake smelled it before we saw it. He hit the water running, and with the great splash there also arose two mallards, drake and hen, to wing off quacking in indignation. Jake watched them thoughtfully as he swam. They circled the pond twice before sloping off to the swamp at the base of the ridge.

I recalled pounding up this same ridge years ago with Luke on a foggy fall afternoon, both of us breathing hard after a long, fruitless hunt, and then Luke getting birdy as we neared the pond. From its brushy edge he flushed two woodcock, both of which I dropped. As he brought them to me, the fog broke and simultaneously I heard celestial chords—I believe the hymn was "Rock of Ages." For a moment I thought I'd died the ideal bird hunter's death—in mid-step, after completing a double—and the Pearly Gates were opening for us both. But then I remembered an item in the local paper saying there would be tryouts that afternoon for a new organist at the Congregational Church in the village, far below. From that day on, I referred to the ridgetop cover as Pearly Gates in my gunning diary.

That summer I also tried to make a fishing dog out of Jake, but it didn't work out—not yet, at least. Simba, my first yellow Lab, used to accompany me on the trout streams, holding at heel while I threw the fly, watching carefully as I played a fish, then picking it up at leader length without ruffling a scale and bringing it to my hand. But Jake thought the point of the exercise was to retrieve the fly, and when I would whisk it away to prevent his getting hooked, he'd dash back along the bank, shake a gallon of ice water over me, and jump at my head just for fun.

He also enjoyed charging upstream ahead of me, flushing trout out of their lies and turning them to dart madly between my legs or take refuge in the lee created by my booted feet. Great technique on grouse, a disaster on brookies. But I haven't given up on him yet as a fishing dog. Once he's outgrown what I call "the scoots"—a young, energetic dog's sudden desire to run as if the devil himself were behind him, zooming often in wide whirlwind circles with his tail down and a naughty-boy glint in his eyes—he

When Jake was nine months old, I tried to make a fishing dog out of him—but he had other ideas . . .

Jake tried to retrieve the fly, and dashed up- and downstream flushing trout. Oh, well . . .

may still settle down enough to go fishing with me without spooking trout.

Luke never took much interest in fishing. He'd follow me along the rivers all right, for a while, but then he'd start hunting the bankside thickets, inevitably finding and flushing game birds. He'd come back to me after the flush and just stand there, a reproachful look in his eyes, then whine softly as if to say, "Why don't you put down that silly stick and get your gun?" Even a live trout, flopping and splashing in the shallows as I unhooked it, did nothing for him. It didn't have feathers.

As the Vermont hunting season approached, I took Jake down to Maryland's Eastern Shore at the beginning of September for his first outing on doves. Never before had I left Luke behind on an

out-of-state bird-hunting expedition, and although I tried to sneak my guns and gear out of the house when I was loading the Jimmy, he knew it. But it would be very hot in Maryland, and I feared that Luke's breathing condition would worsen with the constant panting the heat would provoke. Nonetheless, I felt awful about it. Jake was slowly replacing Luke as my Number-One Dog, just as I'd planned in the cold light of reason, more than a year ago now. And Jake was developing just as I'd hoped he would, learning from Luke and shaping up as a superior gundog. But cold reason is no balm for an aching heart. Still, I wanted Jake to broaden his hunting horizons, to get more experience in socialization with strange people, strange dogs, and an alien landscape. It would make him a better gundog in the years that lay ahead. Luke had never hunted doves. Now Jake would.

Mourning doves are adjudged songbirds by most Northeastern states, but on and below the Mason-Dixon Line the dove season is celebrated by opening-day rites that rank right up there with Jefferson Davis's Birthday—or the white-tailed deer openers in Pennsylvania or Michigan. Joe Judge, a friend of mine from Centreville, Maryland, had invited us to his Pioneer Point Farm on Corsica Neck and the Chester River, a 1,643-acre sprawl of sunflower, soybean, and corn fields surrounded by marshland, for the first dove shoot of the year—a celebratory warm-up for the more serious duck and goose shooting that would follow as the weather cooled.

Jake got along well with everyone, engaging in loud barking matches with Joe's Chesapeake Bay retrievers, Amigo and Maddie Hayes, avoiding his combative Jack Russell terrier, Boomer, who would gladly have bitten his nose off, and frisking in puppylike glee with an elderly houseguest: a stone-deaf, carefully coiffed fourteen-year-old bichon frise named Monet—a white toy poodle look-alike—who seemed a bit overwhelmed by Jake's enthusiasm. In the dove field, he lay at my feet in a cornstalk blind, watched the doves whip past, stayed calm as shotguns boomed around him, and then retrieved like a veteran, plowing his way into matted thistles and bindweed to fetch fallen birds without hesitation.

"You've got a good dog there," Joe said after shooting over him one afternoon in the sunflower fields. "He's got all the promise in the world. Bring him back down for ducks and geese."

Jake was a good companion on the road as well, spending most of his time in his portable kennel but now and then coming up to the front seat with me to gaze solemnly at the eighteen-wheelers as they bellowed by on the Jersey Turnpike. Eight hours in the car each way with no complaints.

Jake picked up right where he'd left off when Vermont's upland season opened on the last Saturday of September. He and Luke were a perfect team, never crowding one another, each of them quartering well within gun range to either side of me as we zig-zagged through the covers. Luke had gotten a new lease on life. The psychological boost provided by the companionship and com-petition from Jake revitalized his whole bearing, and physically, as well, his life had improved. That spring, at Jean Ceglowski's sug-gestion, I had taken him north to Burlington, Vermont, where Dr. Paul Howard, a veterinary surgeon, performed throat surgery to ease Luke's breathing problems. He removed Luke's paralyzed vocal cords to open a wider passage in his larynx. He couldn't bark anymore, of course, but he certainly could breathe more easily. I had left him at Dr. Howard's clinic overnight, expecting to find a very weak dog on my hands the following day, but when I picked him up the next morning he seemed five years younger —he positively pranced to the car and jumped in, eager to be back to the chase. Though his arthritis had worsened, he hunted almost as well as ever that fall.

Indeed, it was one of the best seasons of dog work I've ever had. Not since the days of Max and Simba had I fielded two such cooperative hunting partners. The only trouble I had was keeping alert to both of them at once. On a couple of occasions, they put up woodcock simultaneously, some fifteen yards apart. I missed both birds each time. But I couldn't fault the dogs for that. And anyway, the older I get, the more I hunt for the dog work and the opportunities. The kill is incidental—desirable, but not essential. Hunting is a process, not an end.

It's certainly not the most important thing to Jake, a far more social dog than old Luke, whose whole life had been dedicated to hunting. Jake's a handsome devil and he knows it. In the course of our travels—and he's logged more car miles in his scant two years than Luke did in thirteen—he's had a number of matrimonial proposals from the owners of Lab females in locales as various as

Georgia, Maryland, Wisconsin, and Connecticut. One of them, a magnanimous "father of the bride" type, even offered to pay Jake's airfare to the nuptials. I think he's still too young for such a step, yet Jake is clearly taken with the fairer sex. When my friend Jim Fergus dropped in last fall from Idaho for a few days of Eastern upland shooting, he brought Sweetzer, his yellow Lab female, then two years old, along with him. They'd been hunting their way around the country for a book Jim was writing, a kind of updated, American version of Turgenev's *A Sportsman's Sketches*. Jake was smitten with Sweetz, chasing her around the yard for half an hour, then further demonstrating the depth of his feelings by knocking her flat with a shoulder block. Luke, watching these youthful antics with a barely concealed disdain, finally had had enough and went in the house for a quiet nap. Jake and Sweetz settled down in a

In the fall, Jake had a visitor, a female yellow Lab from Idaho named Sweetz. I could see there was still a lot of puppy in him—in Sweetz, too, although she was almost three.

while to a peaceful game of tug-of-war with a convenient windfall maple branch. Of course, Jake's attraction to Sweetzer wasn't really sexual. She wasn't in heat, and in fact she'd already been spayed. Their mutual infatuation was simply that of young dogs for playmates. Just another example of the youthful high spirits which Labs retain well into middle age, and which makes them such wonderful companions.

Jake and I returned to Joe Judge's place on the Eastern Shore later that fall for his first experience of waterfowling—the game Labradors are traditionally bred for. And if Jungian principles can be applied to dogs, he certainly seemed to have a "racial" memory of duck and goose hunting: it was as if he'd been there before, often, and through many generations.

Joe parked his truck at the edge of the water, and we walked into darkness with Jake at heel, the wind howling at thirty knots out of the north. Spartina grass thrashed and waves pounded the shore. We hiked the barrier beach protecting the marsh with surf booming on the rocks, sloshing and foaming around our feet— cold as the gunmetal dawn just breaking. Jake paused beside the johnboat that would carry us to the blind. He'd never been in a boat before, and I was afraid he might balk at the unfamiliarity of it, but he jumped aboard at my hand signal. He seemed to know that silence was important—no whining, no anxious barking like that so often heard from overeager young duck dogs. The blind, too, was unfamiliar territory, but he walked in as if it were home, then lay at my feet as I sat on the bench and loaded the shotgun. He shivered slightly against my legs as the shells snicked home. He seemed to know what was coming.

And it came quickly. Across the bay I could see a cloud of ducks rise as the light strengthened, their gabbling reaching a crescendo as they took off for their morning feeding. Joe Judge, crouched beside the blind, watching and waiting with his duck call, said, "Okay, get ready. Here they come." He began to call—plaintive, urgent, enticing duck talk that seemed to emanate from the big spread of decoys bobbing in front of the blind. I could hear the whistle of wings, getting stronger as the flight neared us. Jake was shivering all over now, shuddering hot against my legs. Even his eyebrows were shivering, but he kept his head down, eyes averted from the first ducks that raced overhead and circled back into the decoys. Looking up, I could see them, wings cupped, legs extended for the landing. The sky was filled with duck voices.

"Now," Joe said.

We rose and the dawn was dark with birds: fully three hundred mallards and baldpates dropping into the set. The guns banged; ducks fell; ejected shells rattled against the reed walls of the blind. It was over in seconds. Jake still lay at my feet, waiting for the word.

"Good shooting," Joe said. "All right, let Jake out."

I opened the back door of the blind. Jake was out in a hot yellow flash. He turned immediately toward the water, head up, marking down the dead birds.

"Okay, Jake." Joe made an underarm casting motion toward the water. "Fetch!"

He hit the water running, a big, powerful animal doing what he was born to do, and swam strongly through the breaking waves, through the decoys—pausing only once to grab at one, but instantly rejecting it—out to the first of the dead birds bobbing in the water. He grabbed it, turned, and came swimming back, head high, bulling through the heavy weed growth as if it weren't there. He ran up the shore, dropped the bird at Joe's feet, and looked up, awaiting his next orders. Joe cast him off again . . .

My eyes were blurred. Maybe it was the wind. But I doubt it.

Jake brought in twenty-five ducks that weekend, both dead and cripples, and did not maul one of them. He was as tender-mouthed with waterfowl as with upland game. His only problem came later that fall, with Canada geese. Running out from a field blind, he picked up a wounded Canada by the root of its wing and began to drag it back to us. But its ungainly weight pulled him around in circles, and the retrieve was accomplished in a series of loops. Joe and I showed him how to grasp the bird firmly across the back, pinning its wings, and the next time out of the blind he did it correctly.

"I think you've got a winner," Joe said, rumpling Jake's ears. Jake just looked up and smiled.

Old Luke died the following spring. A sudden cancer, but one that apparently caused him little pain. He was thirteen years old, and he'd had a good run in the course of his life. He'd gone the

When I took him down to Maryland for his first Canada goose hunt, Jake showed what Luke and I had taught him. His work was superb. But then he took a well-earned rest.

distance with style and enthusiasm. It's hard for me to realize he's dead. Now and then I still hear him scratching at the back door, asking to be let in. But it's only the wind in the trees.

For days after his death, every time I let him out, Jake hunted the fields behind the house, looking for Luke. I walked with him, sometimes, with tears in my eyes. "He's not there, boy. He's gone away."

Soon afterward Dan Gerber called. "I'm sorry to hear about Luke," he said. "Why don't you and Jake come out here for a visit—kind of a family reunion? Willa tells me she misses him, and I'd like to see how he's turned out."

It would take Jake's mind off Luke's absence, I thought, and perhaps ease my heart as well. So we jumped in the Jimmy and headed west one morning. It was early June and the country was green again. Jake sat beside me this time, enjoying the scenery, a seasoned traveler by now and a boon companion. Sixteen hours in a car was nothing to him. We pulled into Dan's about midnight, and he came out of the house to greet us. Willa came, too, and it was as if brother and sister had never been apart. They took off into the night, running broad circles around the back forty, zooming through the beech trees and ground cover at breakneck speed—an extended yellow blur that zigzagged like chain lightning into and out of the dark.

"Are you butter yet?" Dan asked them, mildly, as they swept past. Then they took to leaping over each other as they ran, an ecstasy of explosive joy. "You're not dogs," Dan told them on their next flyby. "You're land porpoises, that's what you are."

Later, their energies expended for the moment, they lay side by side in the house as they had when they were puppies. Willa was a bit smaller than Jake and had a dark yellow band across the bridge of her nose, linking her eyes like the indentation a pair of glasses leaves on a person's face, but otherwise you couldn't tell them apart except by the color of their collars. When they looked up at us, their faces wore the same expression: alert, curious, eager for something (anything!) new to happen. The genius of the gene pool . . .

Another distinguishing feature, when they were moving slowly enough to see it, was the small spot of black fur growing on Jake's upper lip—a hint of the dominant black coloration in the Labrador

breed, Saint Hubert's hound reminding us of his role in the equation. When Jake was a puppy, the shape of the spot had reminded Dan of a woodcock in flight. A good omen, he'd said, and Jake had fulfilled its promise by becoming an excellent woodcock hunter.

I told Dan about Jake's hunting exploits, and he retaliated with tales of Willa's intellectual attainments. "I read her everything I write," he said, "and she listens with perfect attention, especially to anything dealing with dogs. And she never criticizes—that's the best part. She watches television with me and especially wildlife

When Luke died the next spring, Jake was lonely. I took him to Dan Gerber's house in Michigan for a reunion with his sister, Willa. My, how they'd grown.

films. Her favorite movie on the VCR is *Old Yeller*. She can watch it over and over again and never gets bored. And she barks along with the sound track. She tells me her favorite scene is when Old Yeller tackles the wild boar—she'd like to try that herself some-time, wouldn't you, girl?"

Both dogs looked up, cocked their heads, smiled, and panted their agreement. Then we all went to bed.

Hogan, the third puppy in Jake and Willa's litter, came for a visit with his owners, Lynn and Jerry Zandbergen. I'd never met Hogan before. A bit more subdued than Jake and Willa, he none-theless was indistinguishable from them in looks and bearing. Once again we had yellow dogs threatening to melt into butter as they raced round and round the property. Dan threw tennis balls for them until his arm began to hurt, and they all retrieved impeccably. I noticed, during one of their infrequent rest periods, that Hogan had a dark spot on his tongue (now lolling out about a foot from his mouth)—another evidence of Saint Hubert's blessing, just like Jake's woodcock birthmark and Willa's eyeglasses.

But alike as the three littermates were physically, each had a dis-tinctive personality. Neither Willa nor Hogan was a gundog. Jake was, and he seemed more focused as a result. His confidence and concentration had been formed as much by Luke's teaching as by his genetic heritage. He had Luke's soul now. That fact was brought home to me shortly after we returned from Michigan.

Dan had told me that a mutual friend, the poet and novelist Jim Harrison, had recently lost his thirteen-year-old black Lab female, Sand, just as I had lost Luke. "Jim buried her with a grouse at her head, a woodcock at her feet, and a deer bone to sustain her down the long Ghost Road." It was a touching gesture, and Luke deserved as much himself.

Jake and I would conduct our own symbolic farewell service for Luke, here in the green hills of Vermont.

One day we hiked to the top of the ridge, to the cover I call Pearly Gates. While Jake watched, I scraped out a hole near the edge of the pond and buried Luke's old, faded collar, arrayed with all his dog tags and his hunting bell. I thought of all the birds he'd put up in the course of his life, all the birds for whom the sound of that approaching, inexorable bell had spelled the finish. Now it was silent.

We walked back down the hill, with Jake quartering ahead of me the way Luke had taught him: down through the flowering thorn apples, scrambling over the spilled, lichen-grown stone walls, his own hunting bell clanging, down toward the edge of the swamp. Then Jake got birdy. His tail came up, beating fast, then faster. His head was up, too, nostrils flared, mouth open as he sucked in the bird scent, head weaving slightly to zero in on its source. His

It was hard to tell the three littermates apart, especially when they were moving. That's Willa on top, Hogan next, and Jake on the bottom.

feet took him, almost unbidden, toward a clump of whippy doghair aspen. But as he neared it, he paused for an instant, then circled out and around—just as Luke had taught him. He pushed into the aspens from the far side, to flush the bird back in my direction.

A grouse came pouring out of the cover in a stuttering roar of wings, directly toward me.

I raised an imaginary shotgun, swung through the elongated blur of the bird at speed, hit the imaginary trigger. "Bang!" I said. The bird flew on, but my inner eye saw it puff and tumble, primaries groping like fingers for a grip on the air. My inner ear heard it thud on the ground. Jake was out of the cover, standing at my legs. I could feel his heart thump, and his eyes were locked like mine onto the same empty piece of sky into which the grouse had vanished.

Luke lives.

God bless you, Saint Hubert, wherever you are.

When we got back home, Jake and I paid a visit to "Pearly Gates," one of Luke's best covers, and buried his hunting collar. But Luke's essence lives on now in Jake.